EMBARRASSING GEORGE

Kimber Morgan

For George III, who attempts
to always like my cooking.

@2022 Creative, Simple Wonder Press
All rights reserved.
This book or any portion therof may not be produced or used in any manner without the express written persmission of the publisher.
ISBN: 978-1-7370386-4-1
kimberfoxmorgan.com

EMBARRASSING GEORGE

Written by Kimber Morgan   Illustrated by Jessica Kwan

Samantha's uncle thinks he is a real superhero.

Dorothy's stepmom's brain is the size of a marble.
(At least that's what her brother said.)

Archie thinks his sister is going to be famous because she can touch her toes to her head.

My family isn't going to be famous for anything.

Everyone calls me Little George. "It's a great family name passed down for generations," they tell me. I'm like the 6th or 7th George.

We aren't Kings of England, so they could have stopped counting, and I could just be George.

Or Max. Easy enough.

My sister Jenny walks around making gross kissy faces to her phone all day. My mom says all the teenage girls do it and to just ignore her.

So embarrassing.

My little brother, Teddy, has been wearing his ninja costume day and night for a week now.

Weirdo.

Last week my dad hollered at Archie and me to be quiet. We were OUTSIDE! Where we CAN be loud! And he was in his UNDERWEAR.

Beyond embarrassing.

It's Family Night at school and Teddy is wearing a starfish costume. Mom made it for Halloween last year.
His underwear is showing in the back.

Jenny won't put her phone on mute because she's recording a video.

Mom is complaining that we don't appreciate her cooking.

Even Dad had a hot dog tonight.

When we get to school, Dorothy's stepmom is wearing a ridiculous hat.

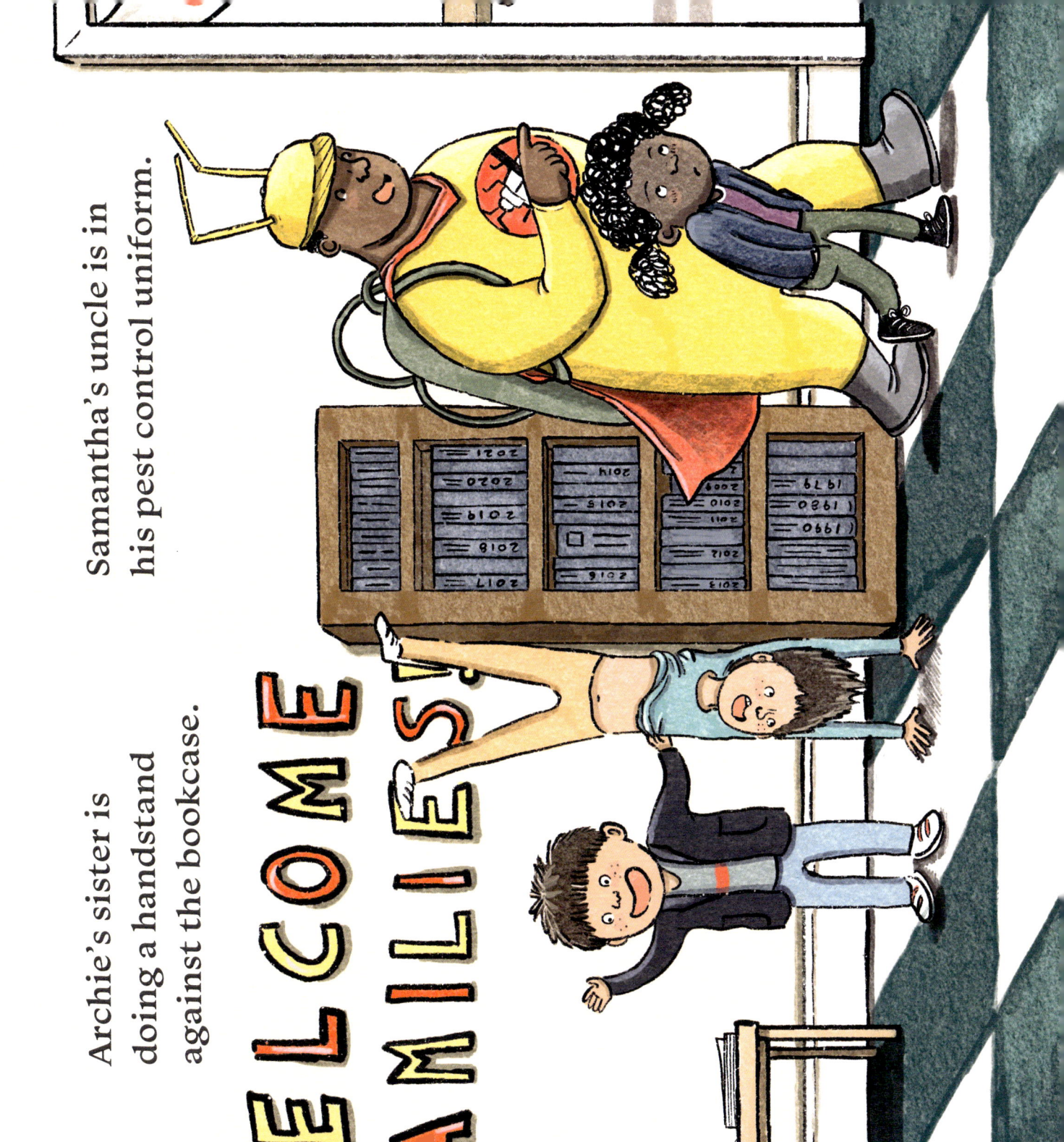

Samantha's uncle is in his pest control uniform.

Archie's sister is doing a handstand against the bookcase.

I hold my breath, hoping I didn't have to hide.

Miraculously... my family is acting normal and just looking at my work.

Am I dreaming?

Teddy is playing with my erasers and Jenny is laughing at my family drawing.

My mom hugs me tight, and my dad gives me a fist bump.

I guess they are impressed with what the 6th or 7th Little George can do.

I smile. We might not become famous one day, but family is family. Everyone is weird and embarrassing sometimes.

Even me.